LONDON, NEW YORK, MUNICH, MELBOURNE, and DELHI

Senior designer Gemma Fletcher
Senior editor Carrie Love
US editor Margaret Parrish
Designer Elaine Hewson
Photographer Dave King
Home economist Denise Smart
Production editor Raymond Williams
Production controller Ché Creasey
Jacket designer Rosie Levine
Managing editor Penny Smith
Managing art editor Marianne Markham
Creative director Jane Bull
Category publisher Mary Ling

First American Edition, 2014
Published in the United States by
DK Publishing
4th floor, 345 Hudson Street
New York, New York 10014

17 18 19   10 9 8 7 6
055-196499-02/14

A catalog record for this book
is available from the Library of Congress.
ISBN: 978-1-4654-1690-2

Printed in China

Discover more at
www.dk.com

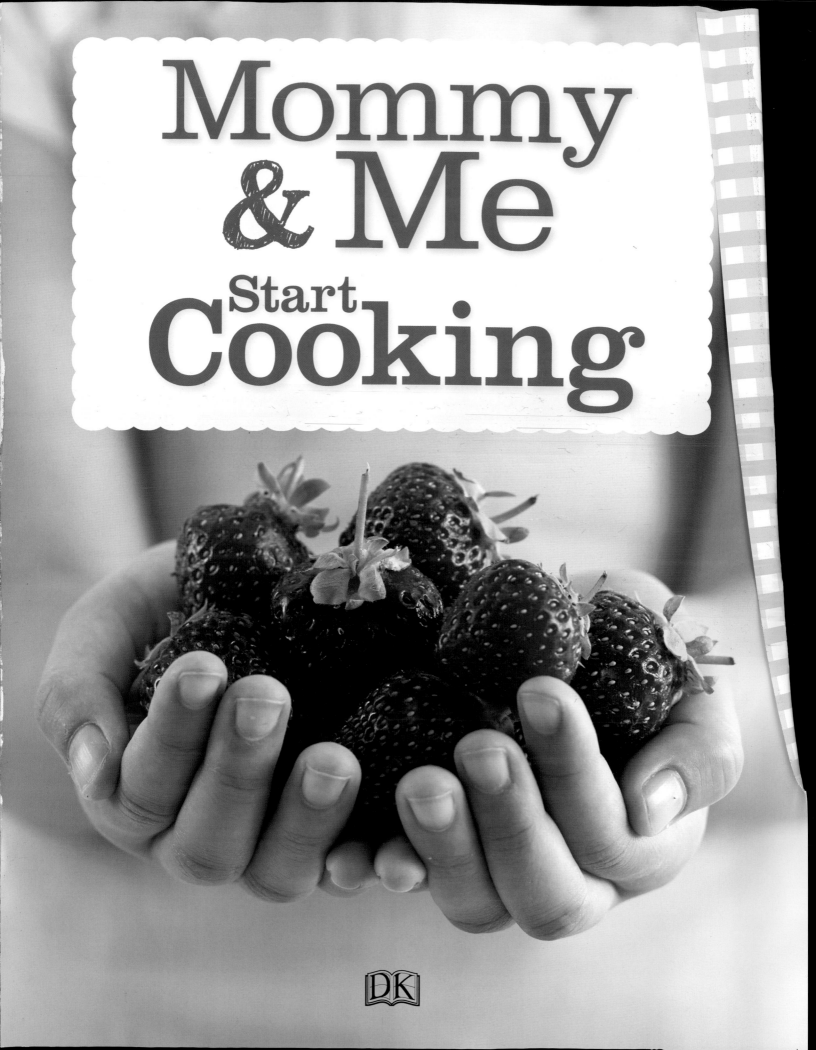

Mommy & Me
Start Cooking

DK

Contents

Health and safety

In this book you will discover the basics about popular ingredients such as eggs and chocolate. You'll find out where they come from and how to cook with them. Always be careful in the kitchen and follow all instructions.

⚠️ Safety

All the projects in this book are to be made under adult supervision. When you see the warning triangle take extra care, since hot stoves, electric appliances, and sharp implements are used to make a recipe. Ask an adult to help.

Getting started

1 Read the instructions all the way through before you start.
2 Gather together everything you need so it's all in one place.
3 Have a cloth handy to mop up any spills.
4 Put on an apron and tie back your hair.

Key to symbols

Food wise

• When you're in the kitchen you should ask an adult to take things in and out of the oven and to use the stovetop.
• Wash your hands before and after you work with food. Always wash your hands after handling raw eggs and raw meat.
• Do not lick your fingers after you've worked with food.
• Check the use-by date on all ingredients.
• The dessert-type recipes are meant to be special treats within a balanced diet.
• Carefully measure the ingredients before you start a recipe or project. Use measuring spoons and cups, and a measuring cup, as necessary.
• Follow the packaging instructions that indicate how to store food.

prep time

cooking time

yield (serves or makes)

Measurements

US measures	Metric measures	Spoon measures
oz = ounce	g = gram	tsp = teaspoon
lb = pound	ml = milliliter	tbsp = tablespoon
fl oz = fluid ounce		

Ask an adult to take hot dishes
in and out of the oven.

Healthy eating

You need to eat a balanced diet made up of a variety of different foods so that you can grow, stay healthy, and have lots of energy for life.

Pasta

Grains

Bread, cereals, rice, and pasta provide energy. They are all grains, or are made from grains. It's better if you eat the whole-grain varieties, since these are rich in minerals and fiber.

Pita bread

Fruits

Your body can get important vitamins and minerals, as well as fiber, from fruits. Fresh, frozen, canned, or dried— all fruits are good for you.

Strawberry

Banana

Vegetables

Vegetables are a very important part of a healthy diet. Like fruits, they are full of vitamins, minerals, and fiber. You should eat a variety of vegetables every day.

Broccoli

Carrots

Kidney beans

Meat and beans

We get protein from both animal and plant sources: meat, fish, nuts and seeds, beans, and dairy products. It's healthy to eat a mixture of all of these.

Salmon

Milk products

Dairy items provide valuable vitamins and minerals (such as calcium). Dairy produce includes milk, yogurt, cheese, butter, cream, and cottage cheese.

Milk

Cheese

Fats and oils

Everyone needs fat for energy and for their bodies to work well. The right type of fat is found in olive oil, nuts, seeds, avocados, and oily fish.

Olive oil

Walnuts

Sugary foods and salt

Sugar gives you energy, but eating too much can be bad for you. Too much salt is also linked with health problems.

Cookies

7

What is an egg?

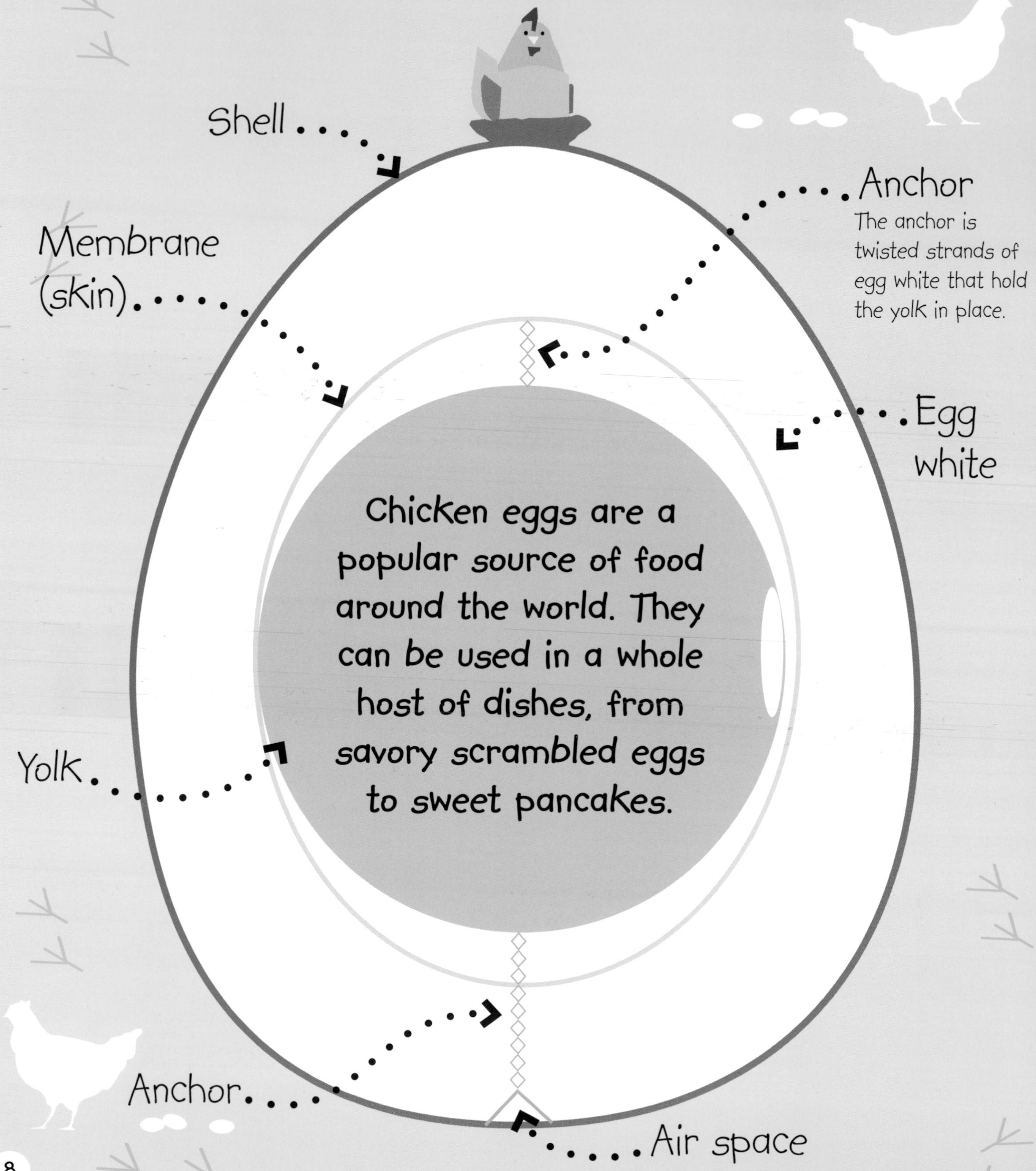

Shell

Membrane (skin)

Anchor
The anchor is twisted strands of egg white that hold the yolk in place.

Egg white

Chicken eggs are a popular source of food around the world. They can be used in a whole host of dishes, from savory scrambled eggs to sweet pancakes.

Yolk

Anchor

Air space

Eggs contain 75 percent water and 12.5 percent protein. The rest is made up of vitamins, minerals, fat, and salt.

A chicken can lay up to 259 eggs in one year.

A chicken starts to lay eggs when she's 19 weeks old.

EGGS ARE FULL OF VITAMINS THAT HELP YOUR BODY STAY HEALTHY.

Which do you prefer? The yolk or the white?

Which is your favorite egg to eat?

Chicken egg (brown)

Chicken egg (white)

Duck egg

Quail egg

9

Eggs and ham

2 mins 5 mins 1

Scrambled eggs are delicious on their own or as part of a hot breakfast. You can increase the flavor of the dish by adding ham to your scrambled eggs.

You will also need:
• Small pat of butter
• Pinch of salt and freshly ground black pepper

Tools:
• Small bowl
• Fork
• Small frying pan
• Wooden spoon

I tbsp milk

1 large egg

Serve with a slice of buttered toast

1oz (30g) chopped ham

You can add fried mushrooms instead of ham.

1 In a small bowl, use a fork to whisk together the egg and milk. Season with salt and pepper.

2 Melt the butter in the pan over medium heat. Add the egg mixture. Using the wooden spoon, stir continuously until the eggs are just set and still creamy.

3 Mix the chopped ham into the eggs. Serve on top of a slice of buttered toast.

Pancakes

5 mins | 12-15 mins | 4 (makes 12)

Pancakes are a wonderful treat for breakfast or perfect as a dessert after a light meal. They're incredibly simple and fun to make.

1 cup self-rising flour

1 tsp baking soda

Baking soda makes the pancakes rise slightly so that they're fluffy.

You can also use all-purpose flour, but you'll need to add 1 tsp of baking powder to it.

You will also need:

• Sunflower oil for frying

Tools:

• Strainer
• Large mixing bowl
• Pitcher
• Fork
• Whisk
• Large nonstick frying pan
• Spatula

3/4 cup milk

You can use whole or skim milk.

1 egg

Yummy toppings to try on your pancakes

Slices of strawberries

Slices of banana

Thinly slice a banana and layer the slices on a pancake before you drizzle syrup on top.

Maple syrup
Blueberries
Confectioner's sugar

⭐1 Sift the flour and baking soda into the bowl and make a well in the center.

⭐2 Using a fork, lightly beat the egg and milk together in the pitcher and pour into the well. Whisk the mixture until you have a smooth batter.

⭐3 Ask an adult to heat a tbsp of oil in a frying pan. Drop large spoonfuls of the batter into the pan.

⭐4 Cook the pancakes for 2 minutes, or until golden on the bottom and with bubbles on the top. Flip over to cook the other side.

⭐5 Carefully slice the bananas and strawberries with a table knife. Serve the pancakes with the fruit and maple syrup.

Try out different fruits or serve with slices of bacon instead.

If you don't like syrup you can use confectioner's sugar. Sprinkle it over the pancakes and fruit.

What is flour?

Wheat has been grown for thousands of years. It is ground into a powder called flour. Flour is the key ingredient for making bread, pastries, cakes, cookies, and pasta. The main types of flour are: white, whole-wheat, self-rising, and bread.

Spikelet......

Beard......

Stem......

......Leaf

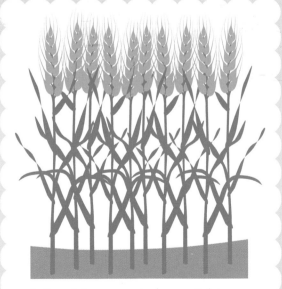

Wheat is grown in large fields. It is a strong type of grass. Each plant yields between 20-50 kernels of grain.

This diagram shows a close-up of the head (or spike) of a wheat plant. Wheat spikes are made up of a number of spikelets, each of which bear one to five flowers. The flowers turn into kernels.

Modern farmers use combine harvesters to harvest (collect) their wheat.

The grain exits the harvester from the chute at the back, usually into a wagon.

The blades in the cutter bar cut down the wheat. It goes up into the machine on a conveyor belt.

The grain is separated from the chaff and straw by a thresher.

Once harvested, grain is taken to a factory where it is ground into flour. The flour is then packaged and sold in stores.

To make it last longer, flour should be stored in a cool, dry, dark place.

1 tsp ground ginger....

You can use a teaspoon of ground cinnamon if you don't like ginger.

2 cups all-purpose flour, sifted

Finely grated zest of 1 orange....

1 medium egg, lightly beaten

Follow the steps on the next page to see which ingredients you put into the bowl first.

Tools:
- 2 large baking sheets
- Parchment paper
- Large mixing bowl
- Wooden spoon
- Rolling pin
- Star-shaped cookie cutters
- Cooling rack
- Small bowl

To decorate:
- 2½ cups confectioner's sugar
- 2-3 tbsp water
- 2-3 drops food coloring

1 Ask an adult to preheat the oven to 350°F (180°C). Line 2 baking sheets with parchment paper. In a bowl, rub the flour and butter together until they resemble bread crumbs.

2 Mix in the sugar, ginger, and orange rind. In a small bowl, beat the egg and corn syrup with a fork, then add to the mixture. Stir with a wooden spoon until it forms a ball.

3 Wrap in plastic wrap and chill in the fridge for 10 minutes. Roll out the dough on a floured surface to ¼in (4–5mm) thickness. Cut into stars using cookie cutters (see pages 22–23).

4 Place the stars slightly apart on the baking sheets and bake for 10–12 minutes, until golden. Let cool on the trays for 2 minutes, then transfer to a cooling rack.

5 Sift the confectioner's sugar into a mixing bowl and slowly stir in enough water to create a smooth mixture. Divide into 3 bowls. Stir in the colorings to make 3 different icings.

6 Carefully spread the icing onto the cookies using a knife or drizzle it on top using a teaspoon or piping bag to create stripes and patterns. Set aside until the icing sets.

 If you prefer, try lemon rind instead of orange.

You can place the
cookie cutters up to
the edge of the dough.

Reroll the extra
trimmings to make
more stars.

Dust the cookie cutters with flour.

Dust the rolling pin with flour to prevent sticking.

Flour

Blueberry cake

Sponge cakes are ideal for birthdays or other special occasions. They can be filled with the fruit of your choice. We've chosen juicy blueberries.

4 tbsp blueberry jam or preserves

½ cup heavy cream

6oz (175g) blueberries

Reserve a handful, to decorate the top of the cake.

Confectioner's sugar, to dust.

24

2 cups
confectioner's sugar

20
mins

25
mins

8-10

Tools:
- 2 x 8in (20cm) round cake pans
- Scissors and parchment paper
- Large mixing bowl
- Electric hand mixer
- Strainer
- Large metal spoon
- Wire cooling rack
- Medium mixing bowl
- Whisk

Use butter at room temperature, instead of straight from the refrigerator. It will be easier to beat into the mixture.

16 tbsp
softened butter

2 cups
self-rising
flour

4 large eggs,
lightly beaten

1 Ask an adult to preheat the oven to 350°F (180°C). Draw around the pan twice on the parchment paper and cut out. Grease the parchment paper and line both pans.

2 Place the butter and sugar in a large mixing bowl and beat with the electric mixer until light and creamy.

3 Add a little of the eggs and beat in. Repeat until all the egg mixture has been added.

4 Sift the flour into the mixture. Use a metal spoon to fold it together until all the flour has disappeared.

5 Divide the mixture between the pans, leveling the tops with the back of the spoon. Bake for 25 minutes, or until risen and firm to the touch.

6 Leave to cool briefly in the pans, then turn onto a wire rack to cool. Remove the parchment paper and allow the cakes to cool completely.

For an alternative filling, you can use sliced strawberries instead of blueberries.

Finishing touches

Whip the cream in a bowl using the whisk, until it forms soft peaks. Spread the flat side of one cake with jam, then top with whipped cream and blueberries. Place the other cake on top. To decorate, add a handful of blueberries and sift confectioner's sugar over the top.

Serve the cake in slices of equal size.

Cheesy bread rolls

These bread rolls are simple and fun to make. The melted cheese on top of each roll adds a lot of flavor to the bread. You can eat the rolls plain or fill them with sandwich fillings.

2 cups strong white bread flour

1½ cups tepid water......

......2 tsp active dry yeast

2 hours 20 mins | 25-30 mins | 9

1 tsp sugar

2 cups whole-wheat bread flour

Whole-wheat bread flour contains tiny bits of grain that give the bread an interesting texture.

Ingredients to serve:

- 9 lettuce leaves
- 2 tomatoes, sliced
- 5 slices ham
- 4 slices Cheddar cheese

Tools:

- Small bowl
- Teaspoon
- Large mixing bowl
- Wooden spoon
- Clean dish towel
- Large baking sheet
- Pastry brush

1½ tsp salt

Items to top your rolls with before baking

⅔ cup grated sharp Cheddar cheese

1 egg, beaten

1 Pour ½ cup of the water into a small bowl. Sprinkle in the yeast and sugar and stir until dissolved. Let stand in a warm place for 5 minutes, or until *bubbles* appear on the surface.

2 Put both types of flour and the salt into a large bowl and use a spoon to mix together. Use your hand to make a well in the center.

3 Pour the yeast and most of the remaining water into the well and gently mix together to form a soft dough. Stir in the extra water if it is too dry.

4 Turn the dough onto a floured surface. Knead firmly using the heel of your hand, folding the dough over as you go. Knead for 10 minutes, until smooth and shiny. Put the dough in a clean bowl and cover with a dish towel. Let rise in a warm place for $1\frac{1}{2}$–2 hours, until doubled in size.

5 Ask an adult to preheat the oven to 425°F (220°C). Punch down the risen dough by punching it with your knuckles.

6 Divide the dough into 9 equal pieces. Dust your hands with a little flour and shape the dough into rolls.

7 Place the rolls on a greased baking sheet, cover with a damp dish towel, and let stand for 10 minutes.

8 Brush the rolls with the egg and press the cheese on top of each roll. Bake for 25–30 minutes, or until risen and golden.

Allow to cool slightly before filling with whatever you like.

What is pasta?

Pasta is made by mixing finely sifted flour, olive oil, and egg. Pasta is produced in factories, but it can also be made at home using a pasta machine or by cutting it by hand to make different types. Pasta is yummy and fills you up!

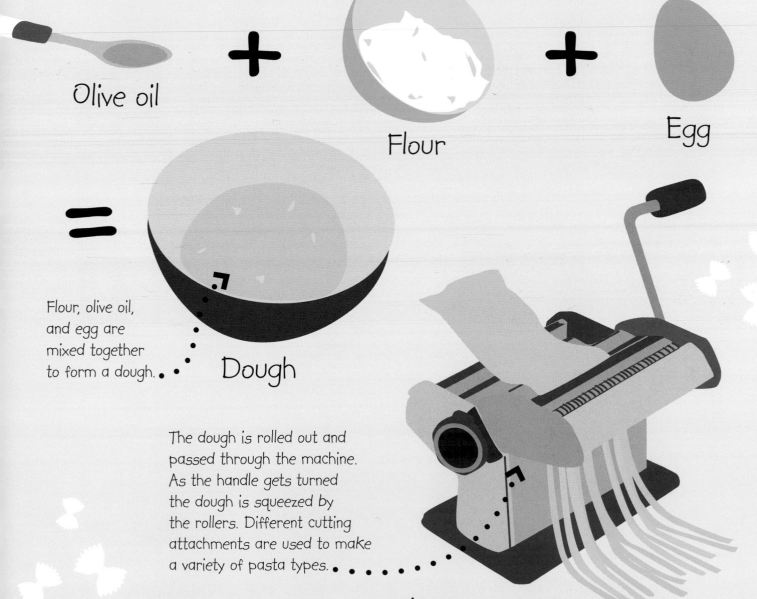

Olive oil **+** Flour **+** Egg

=

Flour, olive oil, and egg are mixed together to form a dough.

Dough

The dough is rolled out and passed through the machine. As the handle gets turned the dough is squeezed by the rollers. Different cutting attachments are used to make a variety of pasta types.

Pasta machine

What is your favorite type of pasta?

Conchiglie rigate
(shell)

Farfalle
(butterfly shape)

Fusilli (twists)

Whole-wheat
penne

Rigatoni (large
grooved tubes)

Macaroni
(narrow tubes)

Penne rigate
(striped quill)

Stelline
(little stars)

Ruote tricolore
(wheels)

Tortiglione
(hollow spiral)

Tortelloni (stuffed with
cheese, meat, or veggies)

Pansotti (pot-bellied
dumplings)

Spinach trottole
(trottole means "spins")

Cappellacci (stuffed
with a pumpkin filling)

Tortelli anolini
(half-moon-shaped bundle)

Vermicelli nest

Cannelloni (stuffed
with sauce and meat)

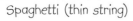
Tagliatelle (thin and
delicate flat noodles)

Spaghetti (thin string)

Lasagne sheets

40 mins (including 10 mins chilling) 10-12 mins 16 (depending on cookie cutters)

Star cookies

These ginger and orange star cookies have a real zing to them. You'll have lots of fun cutting them out of the dough and decorating them with colored icing.

9 tbsp butter, cubed

1 cup confectioner's sugar

Small cubes of butter are easier to rub into flour than a big block.

2 tbsp corn syrup

Cooking pasta

Pasta forms the base of many popular dishes, so it's important you know the right way to cook it. If you don't cook it long enough it is crunchy, and if you overcook it then it becomes soggy!

1 Ask an adult to bring slightly salted water to a boil in a large saucepan.

2 Choose the type of pasta you want for your meal and ask an adult to add the correct quantity to the boiling water. Cook the pasta for 10–12 minutes (or less time if recommended on the package).

Smaller pasta shapes will take less time to cook.

3 Ask an adult to use a slotted spoon to take out a piece for you to test that it's ready. It should be soft, but not soggy. Let the pasta cool before you try it. Ask an adult to pour the pasta into a colander to drain it.

Use warm running water to rinse the pasta. ••••••••

15 mins | 20 mins | 4-6

Pasta bake

This pasta bake makes a perfect healthy family meal. Serve it with a crisp salad to add some greens. The meatballs are super easy and fun to make, and your pasta bake will instantly become a family favorite.

2 tbsp chopped fresh parsley

2 tbsp freshly grated Parmesan cheese

12oz (350g) lean ground beef

You can also make your own bread crumbs by toasting a slice of bread and pulsing it in a food processor.

···· 1 tbsp dried bread crumbs

You will also need:
- Salt and freshly ground pepper
- 1 tbsp olive oil
- 1 good-quantity tomato pasta sauce (see pages 52–53)

To serve:
- Crisp green salad

Tools:
- Large mixing bowl
- Wooden spoon
- Medium saucepan
- Large saucepan
- Large ovenproof dish

4oz (125g) ball mozzarella, drained and roughly chopped ······

····· 1 egg, beaten

9oz (250g) dried rigatoni or penne pasta ·····

1 Place the *beef, egg, parsley, Parmesan,* and *bread crumbs* in the bowl. Season with salt and pepper. Use your hands to combine the mixture.

2 Use your hands to roll the mixture into 24 small balls. Set aside.

3 Ask an adult to cook the pasta in a saucepan of slightly salted boiling water for 10–12 minutes, until tender. Drain well.

4 Ask an adult to heat the oil in a large pan and lightly brown the meatballs in 2 batches. Return all the meatballs to the pan. Add the tomato sauce, cover, and simmer for 5 minutes.

5 Carefully stir the pasta into the meatball mixture, then transfer to the ovenproof dish.

6 Tear the cheese and sprinkle over the top of the dish. Ask an adult to cook it under a preheated broiler for 3–4 minutes, until the cheese has melted. Serve with a salad.

You can substitute ground turkey or pork for the beef to make the meatballs.

What is rice?

Rice is the staple (main) food for almost half the people in the world. It has a mild flavor so it goes with lots of food. It keeps for a long time and when it's cooked it can be sticky or fluffy.

Rice grows in paddy fields that are flooded with water. The water helps to stop weeds from growing in the fields.

Rice has two outer layers. The hull is on the outside, underneath is the bran, followed by the white rice.

White rice

Hull

Bran

Germ

Rice takes about 4 months to grow. It's picked by hand or combine harvester.

White rice has had the bran removed. Brown rice still has its layer of bran.

SHORTGRAIN RICE IS EASY TO EAT WITH CHOPSTICKS BECAUSE THE GRAINS ARE SOFT AND STICK TOGETHER.

Which is your favorite type of rice?

Long grain rice is light and fluffy when cooked.

Basmati rice is used a lot in Indian-style cooking.

Paella rice, as its name suggests, is used to make paellas.

Carnaroli rice is often used to make risottos.

Short grain rice is creamy when cooked and is used for rice puddings.

Despite its name, wild rice isn't actually rice!

10 mins   20 mins   4

Chicken risotto

Risotto dishes use hot stock to soak through and cook the rice, meat, and vegetables. This makes the meal incredibly tasty!

2½oz (75g) low-fat cream cheese

2 tbsp chopped parsley

1 small onion, chopped

2 tbsp freshly grated Parmesan cheese

3 cups hot chicken or vegetable stock

1¼ cups basmati rice

Risottos are usually made with arborio rice, but we have used basmati.

3 boneless, skinless chicken breasts, cubed

½ cup frozen peas

½ cup canned corn, drained

You will also need:
- Small pat of butter
- 1 tbsp sunflower oil

Tools:
- Strainer • Small sharp knife
- Medium saucepan with lid
- Cutting board • Wooden spoon

45

1 Place the rice in a strainer. Rinse the rice under cold running water, until the water runs clear. Drain well.

2 Heat the butter and oil in the saucepan, add the onion, and cook for 2–3 minutes. Stir in the chicken and cook until lightly browned.

3 Add the rice to the pan, stir to coat in the oil, and cook for 1 minute, until the rice is transparent.

4 Add half of the stock and cook over low heat, until most of the liquid has been absorbed, stirring occasionally.

5 Stir in the remaining stock and cook until the stock has been absorbed and the rice is tender; this should take 10–12 minutes. Stir in the peas and corn and cook for 2–3 minutes.

6 Stir in the cream cheese, parsley, and Parmesan cheese. Season to taste and serve in bowls immediately.

Leave out the chicken for a veggie version. Add more vegetables, meat-free sausages, or tofu.

What is a tomato?

A tomato is the fruit of a tomato plant, but in cooking it's always called a vegetable. Tomatoes are used in many ways: as the base for sauces and soups, or as part of a salad. Tomatoes come in several shapes, colors, and sizes.

Node......

Flower

Leaf

Fruit

Shoot

Root

Primary root

Lateral root..

The roots of a tomato plant grow underground and the shoots grow above. Tomato plants need lots of sunshine and water to thrive.

It takes 25 tomatoes to make one bottle of tomato sauce.

Tomatoes are often picked before they are ripe so that they can be transported to retailers before going bad.

The tomato was first eaten in South America, before it became popular globally.

PEOPLE IN ELIZABETHAN ENGLAND THOUGHT TOMATOES WERE BAD FOR YOU. NOW WE THINK THE OPPOSITE.

Vine ripened tomato

Beefsteak tomato

Cherry tomatoes

Yellow tomato

Green zebra tomato

Baby plum tomato

Grape tomatoes

Preparing tomatoes

To make certain recipes you need to know how to get the ingredients ready. Tomatoes can be used in many ways, so it's important to learn how to prepare them properly.

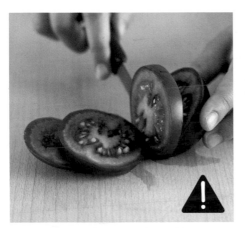

How to slice a tomato

Use a sharp knife to cut the first slice off one end of the tomato. Cut the rest of the tomato into slices of similar thickness.

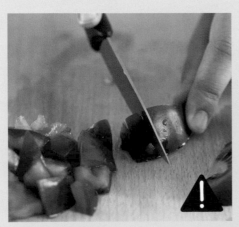

How to cube a tomato

Cut a tomato in half vertically. Slice the halves into wedges of equal size. Then cut each individual wedge into cubes.

How to skin a tomato

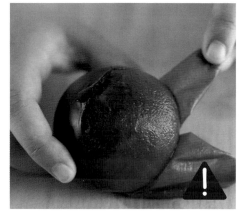

Tomatoes will not ripen in the fridge, so keep them at room temperature for the best color and flavor.

1 Cut a cross on the top of a tomato. Place the tomato in a bowl. Cover with boiling water and leave for 10 seconds.

2 Drain the water from the bowl and place the tomato into a bowl of cold water. When the tomato is cool enough to handle, peel off the skin.

Tomatoes are usually red, but some varieties are yellow or purple.

Tomatoes are amazingly versatile. How will you use yours?

How to seed a tomato

Cut a tomato in half horizontally. Use your fingers to scoop out the seeds and juice over a small bowl.

Tomato sauce

10 mins · 20 mins · 4

Most pasta dishes have a tomato-based sauce. Meat or vegetables are often added to the sauce to create variety, but pasta and tomato sauce are also delicious on their own.

You will also need:
- Salt and freshly ground black pepper
- 1 tsp sugar

Tools:
- Medium saucepan
- Wooden spoon

2 x 14oz (400g) cans chopped tomatoes

1 clove garlic, crushed

2 tbsp tomato paste

Small handful of fresh basil

1 onion, chopped

2 tbsp olive oil

1 Ask an adult to heat the oil in the saucepan over medium heat. Add the onion and garlic and cook for 4–5 minutes, until softened, but not browned.

2 Stir in the tomatoes, tomato paste, and sugar. Bring to a boil, then reduce the heat and simmer, uncovered, for 15 minutes, stirring occasionally.

3 Using your hands, tear the basil leaves into small pieces. Stir into the sauce and season to taste.

Pita pizzas

Pizza sauce is easy to make. Spread one tablespoon of it on a pita bread (that's been toasted for a minute). Add grated mozzarella and any other toppings you like. Ask an adult to broil it for five minutes.

To make the pizza sauce, you will need:

- 1 cup tomato sauce
- 2 tbsp tomato paste
- ½ tsp sugar
- 1 tsp mixed dried herbs
- Small saucepan
- Wooden spoon

10 mins
15 mins
4

Place all the ingredients for the sauce in the saucepan. Ask an adult to simmer the sauce over low heat, stirring occasionally, for 5 minutes. Let cool.

For the toppings:

- 4 tbsp pizza sauce (1 tbsp per pita)
- 4 handfuls of grated mozzarella
- 1 slice of ham, cut into strips
- 1 handful of corn
- Slice of pineapple, cut into chunks
- 5 pieces of pepperoni
- 1 slice of green, red, and yellow pepper, diced
- 4 cherry tomatoes, sliced
- 3 fresh basil leaves, to garnish
- 1 handful of chargrilled chicken pieces
- 1 mushroom, sliced and fried
- 4 strips of red pepper

Which pizza toppings will you choose?

Ham, corn, and pineapple

Pepperoni and peppers

Cheese and tomato with basil

Chicken, mushroom, and red pepper

Lay out your ingredients, ready to make your pizzas.

What is a potato?

A potato is a vegetable that grows under the ground. Potatoes come in a variety of types and sizes. They are a popular food around the world and are prepared to eat in a variety of ways.

Flower

Leaflets

Stem

Roots

Underground stem

Developing tuber

Shoots begin to push out of the ground 2–6 weeks after planting. Under the ground, potatoes (called tubers) form.

Fully expanded tuber

Roots

Old seed place

Potatoes can be diced, sliced, cubed, and grated. They can be fried, boiled, mashed, steamed, or baked!

The flower of the potato plant is toxic. Certain types of potato plant produce small green fruits. Don't eat them though—they are poisonous!

The layer just inside the skin is the most nutritious part of the potato. Always use a potato peeler to keep from cutting too deep and losing nutrients.

IN THE US, POTATO PRODUCTS ARE THE SECOND MOST CONSUMED FOOD OVERALL, TRAILING ONLY DAIRY PRODUCTS.

Potatoes are only distantly related to sweet potatoes, which are root vegetables.

Yukon Gold

Russet

Sweet potatoes

New potatoes

Fingerling

Potato fishcakes

Creamy mashed potatoes and salmon covered in crispy bread crumbs make this dish irresistible.

1 tbsp fresh parsley, chopped......⌐

9oz (250g) potatoes, peeled.....⌐

Cut the potatoes into 2in (5cm) pieces.

2 scallions, trimmed and finely chopped.....⌐

2 tsp Dijon mustard

2/3 cup all-purpose flour

60-70 mins | 40 mins | 4

1 1/3 cups dried bread crumbs

You will also need:

- Freshly ground black pepper
- Pinch of salt
- 6 tbsp sunflower oil
- Salad, to serve
- Lemon wedges, to serve

Tools:

- Medium saucepan
- Colander
- Potato masher
- Mixing bowl
- Fork
- Wooden spoon
- Large plate
- Plastic wrap
- Dish
- 2 medium plates
- Large frying pan
- Fish slice
- Paper towels

12oz (350g) canned salmon, drained weight

2 eggs

59

1 Half fill the saucepan with water. Add the potatoes and a pinch of salt. Ask an adult to bring it to a boil and cook for 12–15 minutes.

2 Drain the potatoes in the colander and put them back in the pan. Mash until smooth and let them stand until they are cool enough to handle.

3 Break the salmon into small pieces in a bowl, removing the skin and bones. Stir in the potatoes, mustard, scallions, and parsley. Season.

4 Lightly dust your hands with a little flour and shape the mixture into 8 cakes. Place on a plate, cover with plastic wrap, and chill in the refrigerator for 30 minutes.

5 Beat the eggs. Put the flour and bread crumbs on separate plates. Coat each fishcake in flour, then egg, and then bread crumbs. Ask an adult to preheat the oven to low heat.

6 Ask an adult to heat half the oil in a large pan over medium heat. Shallow fry 4 of the fishcakes for 2–3 minutes on each side, or until golden. Keep them warm in the oven. Repeat with the other fishcakes.

Serve the fishcakes with a wedge of lemon and a mixed-leaf salad.

What is a pea?

Peas are a popular vegetable to grow and eat. There are two main types to try. The garden pea is shelled from its pod before being eaten, but podded peas, such as snow peas or sugar snap peas, are eaten with the pod intact.

Flower

Pea pod

Leaf

Shoot.........

Root.........

Peas grow on vinelike plants. When the flower drops off, a pea pod grows in its place. The peas grow inside the pod until they're ready to pick.

Shelling peas

Press down gently on one end of the pod to open it up.

Use your thumb to push down one side of the pod to reveal the peas.

Use your thumb to push down inside the pod so that all the peas come out.

Peas are green because they are picked before they are ripe. A ripe pea is more yellow than green in color.

Once picked, peas can be kept in the refrigerator or freezer. Only 5 percent of peas picked are sold fresh. Most are frozen or canned.

Sugar snap peas...

Garden pea pods...

Snow peas...

Garden peas

Pea hummus

5 mins   3 mins   6

This pea hummus is incredibly tasty and full of flavor. Packed with protein and vitamins, this dip is perfect as a healthy snack or as a side dish to accompany lunch or dinner.

You will also need:
- Salt and freshly ground black pepper
- Vegetables, to serve

Tools:
- Medium saucepan
- Strainer
- Food processor
- Bowl or 3 paper cups

1 tbsp tahini

Juice of 1 lemon

2 tbsp olive oil

1½ cups frozen peas

14oz (400g) can chickpeas, drained

1 Cook the peas in a saucepan of boiling water for 3 minutes. Carefully drain through a strainer, then refresh under cold water.

2 Place all the ingredients in a food processor and blend until smooth and creamy. Season with salt and pepper. Use a teaspoon to test a small amount. Transfer to a bowl or into two paper cups to serve.

Serve with sliced vegetables such as carrots, peppers, celery, and snow peas.

What is chocolate?

Chocolate is made from cocoa beans, the seeds of the cacao tree, which grows in tropical forests. Cocoa beans were first used to make a bitter drink that was the opposite of the sweet hot chocolate we drink today and the creamy bars we love to eat!

Stem

Outer shell

Cocoa pods grow on the main branches and trunk of the cacao tree. They grow to the size of melons and take 4–5 months to ripen.

The inside of a cocoa bean is called the nib.

White pulp

Cocoa beans

HOW IS MILK CHOCOLATE MADE?

Start with cocoa mass,

then add sugar

followed by whole milk,

add cocoa butter.

Mix everything together

and you get chocolate!

Milk chocolate is the same as dark chocolate, but with milk added.

White chocolate contains cocoa butter, not cocoa mass (ground cocoa beans), so isn't always thought to be true chocolate.

Cocoa powder is made from ground cocoa beans that have had the cocoa butter removed.

Dark chocolate is cocoa mass mixed with sugar and cocoa butter.

67

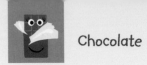

Chocolate truffles

Create these amazing truffles as presents for friends and family. Make 6 gift boxes and put 4 truffles in each box. Everyone will be impressed with how delicious and pretty your truffles are.

1 tbsp
unsalted butter

Make sure you use heavy cream. Light cream is too runny and won't work.

²/₃ cup
heavy cream

5 mins | 125 mins | Makes 24 truffles

Use confectioner's sugar to dust your hands.

You can also make these truffles with milk or dark chocolate.

10oz (300g) white chocolate (30% cocoa)

Make sure you use a bowl big enough to fit all the ingredients.

To decorate:

Choose from
- Sifted cocoa powder
- Grated milk, dark, and white chocolate
- Chocolate pieces
- Sugar sprinkles
- Chopped nuts, e.g., pistachios, roasted hazelnuts
- Shredded coconut

Tools:

- Baking sheet
- Parchment paper
- Medium-sized bowl
- Small saucepan
- Wooden spoon
- Teaspoon
- Strainer

1 Line the baking sheet with parchment paper. Break the chocolate into small pieces in the bowl and set aside. Put the cream in the small saucepan with the butter and ask an adult to bring it slowly to a boil. Then pour the cream over the broken chocolate.

2 With a wooden spoon, stir until the mixture is smooth and all the chocolate has melted. Cover and allow the mixture to cool for about 10 minutes at room temperature. Then transfer to the refrigerator to chill for about 2 hours, until firm enough to handle.

Be creative and come up with other toppings to roll your truffles in.

3 Using a teaspoon, scoop out bite-sized pieces of the chocolate mixture.

4 Dust your hands with powdered sugar so that they don't stick to the chocolate. Roll into balls and place on the baking sheet.

5 Roll the truffles in sifted cocoa powder or grated chocolate, sprinkles, nuts, or coconut. Place in individual baking cups and chill. They will keep for up to 10 days in an airtight container. Store them in the refrigerator because they contain cream.

What's your favorite truffle?

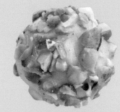

Rolled in chopped
pistachio nuts

Dusted with
cocoa powder

Sprinkled with
shredded coconut

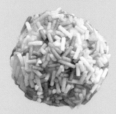

Rolled in dark
chocolate pieces

Covered in
colorful sprinkles

Rolled in grated
milk chocolate

These chocolate truffles
are so delicious they will
melt in your mouth.

20 mins | 2-3 mins | 4

Chocolate dip

Fruit dipped in chocolate is a sweet treat that everyone will like. Make this dish for a party. Everyone can start dipping and share in the chocolatey fun!

You will also need:
- ½ cantaloupe, seeds scooped out (use a melon baller to make balls from the fruit)
- 1 pineapple, sliced into chunks
- 2 mangoes, cubed
- 3 kiwi fruit, sliced

Tools:
- Small saucepan
- Small grater
- Wooden spoon
- Serving bowl
- 2 large plates
- Wooden skewers

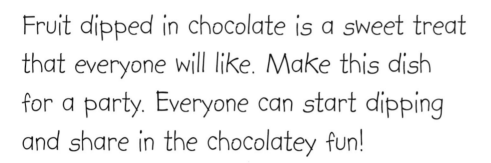

4½oz (125g) good-quality milk chocolate

The chocolate should be 32 percent cocoa. Break it into small pieces.

⅔ cup heavy cream

2 tbsp corn syrup

1 lime

1 Place the chocolate, cream, and corn syrup in the pan and finely grate the rind of the lime over the top.

2 Cook on low heat, stirring until all the chocolate has melted and you have a smooth sauce. Pour into a serving bowl and let cool.

Arrange the fruit onto 2 large plates. Using skewers, dip the fruit in the chocolate dip.

What is a strawberry?

Strawberries are a popular fruit to grow and eat around the world. The sweet flavor, soft texture, and juice content of a strawberry make it perfect for use in drinks, desserts, jams, and sauces.

Flower.

The strawberry fruit grows as the petals fall away.

Fruit

Leaf.

Strawberries need moist growing conditions. They should be planted in dappled shade or in direct sunlight to thrive.

Stem.

Runner

Roots

The garden strawberry that we eat today was first cultivated in France in the 1750s.

A SERVING OF EIGHT STRAWBERRIES CONTAINS MORE VITAMIN C THAN ONE ORANGE.

Strawberries are a traditional dessert served in Sweden on Midsummer's Night (June 23).

Strawberries are the only fruit that have seeds on the outside.

In Roman times, strawberries were used as a medicine.

60,000lb (28,000kg) strawberries are eaten at the annual tennis tournament in Wimbledon, UK.

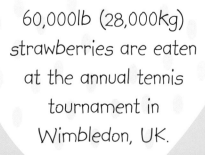

5 mins | 4

Smoothie time

Smoothies make a yummy snack or a tasty breakfast drink. They are easy and quick to make and you can experiment with your own choices of ingredients.

Tools:
- Table knife
- Cutting board
- Blender

1 cup fat-free vanilla yogurt

1 ripe banana

1 cup skim milk

It's important that you rinse strawberries before you eat them.

10oz (300g) strawberries

Hull the strawberries first by taking out the stems.

1 Use a table knife to cut the strawberries in half and set them aside. Peel the banana and roughly chop it into chunks.

2 Carefully place the strawberries and banana in a blender with the vanilla yogurt and the milk. Put the lid on securely. Blend until the mixture is thick and smooth, then pour into glasses. Serve at once.

Freeze your smoothies for a cool treat!

Once you've made your smoothie mixture you can pour it into 4 molds to make delicious ice pops, ready for a hot day.

It's best to drink a smoothie right after it's made. If you let it sit for too long, you'll need to stir it to remix the ingredients.

Index

Acknowledgments

With thanks to: Jennifer Lane for additional editing, Tamsin Weston for additional prop styling, Katie Federico for assisting at a photo shoot, and Jo Casey for proofreading.

Photos courtesy of: Peter Anderson, Philip Dowell, Will Heap, Ian O'Leary, Richard Leeney, Gary Ombler, William Shaw, and Linda Whitwam. All other images © Dorling Kindersley

With special thanks to the models:
Roberto Barney Allen, Abi and Kate Arnold, Lara Duffy, James and Ying Glover, Kathryn Meeker, Ella and Eva Menzie and Oliver Tran.